Spanish Colonialism

and

Diego Fernández de Córdoba

improbablevoices.com

Understanding Spanish Colonialism from the Unusual Perspective of Diego Fernández de Córdoba

Derek Dwight Anderson

Copyright ©2022 Derek Dwight Anderson
All Rights Reserved.

No part of this book may be reproduced or transmitted in any form or by any means, electronic or mechanical, including photocopying, recording, or by any information storage and retrieval system without permission in writing from the author.

ISBN-13: 9798361310128

Cover illustration: "Rapier," Spanish, 17th century, courtesy of the Metropolitan Museum of Art, New York, 14.25.988.

Cataloging Data:

Understanding Spanish Colonialism from the
Unusual Perspective of Diego Fernández de Córdoba /
Derek Dwight Anderson

Sausalito, California

Includes bibliographic references.
Series: Understanding World History Through Biography

1. Spain—Colonies—America—17th century. 2. Fernández de Córdoba, Diego, 1578-1630. 3. Latin America—History—17th century. 4. Mexico—History—17th century. 5. Peru—History—17th Century.

980.013—dc23
LCC F1231.F47

**For additional resources and information visit:
improbablevoices.com**

PREFACE

I remain proud of the 2020 publication of *Improbable Voices: A History of the World Since 1450 Seen from Twenty-Six Unusual Perspectives*, but with the passage of time, I have come to appreciate the fact its length was unwieldy for certain readers. In an effort to make the work more accessible to those who are interested in specific eras, what I consider to be some of the best chapters of *Improbable Voices* are now being published individually. The result is more than a typical introduction to a topic, but this book will not be mistaken by experts as being a comprehensive or definitive work either. Instead, my hope is that motivated students, thoughtful instructors, and general readers who are looking for particular historical case studies will find the books in my Understanding World History Through Biography series to be a useful alternative to other available works.

As was true with *Improbable Voices* as a whole, my goal here is to try to explain an important moment in modern history and to celebrate biography as a genre without focusing upon well-known personalities. This is because lesser-known individuals also shape history just as history shapes people. My overall aim is to provide the reader with sufficient depth to gain an understanding of a life in the context of a particular time and to understand a given era through the experiences of a specific individual.

I retain my indebtedness to dozens of libraries and a multitude of individuals who supported me through the eight-year research, writing and publishing processes. Similarly, I remain steadfast in my dedication: "in honor of my students and great teachers—especially, Marty, Terry, and Valerie."

Words with an asterisk (*) are defined in the glossary on page 43.

Spanish Colonialism and Diego Fernández de Córdoba

In their treatment of Latin America, most world history texts move with astonishing speed from Cortés, Pizarro, and the Conquest in the sixteenth century to Bolívar, San Martín, and Independence in the nineteenth. The period in between, particularly the seventeenth century, stands as something of a lost, untold epoch of Spanish rule in the Americas. But during the 1600s the work of rather cautious government officials like Diego Fernández de Córdoba y López de las Roelas allowed Spain to solidify its lasting cultural impact on Latin America. In doing so, Fernández helped realize Philip II's dream of creating a vast Catholic empire.

Fernández de Córdoba came from a noble family with a long history of serving the Spanish crown. His forefathers led decisive military campaigns against the Moors in Granada, Algeria, and Navarre. Subsequently, they then served important administrative roles in these areas and in Toledo, Córdoba, Italy, and the Low Countries.[1] Diego's uncle, Luis Fernández de Córdoba y Portocarrero, for example, became a key ecclesiastical figure, serving as bishop to Salamanca and Málaga and as archbishop to Santiago de Compostela and Seville.[2]

Fernández's family background and his being a cousin[3] to King Philip III gave him the *entrée* to the Spanish court as a young man. His first major assignment for the crown came in 1598, when he traveled to Graz, Austria as the personal representative of the Spanish king.[4] Fernández's mission was to escort fifteen-

---

[1] For detailed information on the family, see Yuen-Gen Liang, *Family and Empire: The Fernández de Córdoba and the Spanish Realm* (Philadelphia, Pennsylvania: University of Pennsylvania Press, 2011), especially pages 1-7.
[2] Sarai Pérez Herrera, "Linaje, Poder y Cultura De La Nobleza De Guadalcázar. Aproximación Al Eclesiástico Luis Fernández De Córdoba y Portocarrero/Lineage, Power and Culture of the Guadalcázar Nobility. Approximation to the Ecclesiastic Luis Fernández of Córdoba y Portocarrero." *Anales De Historia Del Arte* 23, (2013): 419-427, ProQuest Central. Luis Fernández de Córdoba y Portocarrero (1555-1625) was bishop of Salamanca from 1602 to 1615; bishop of Málaga from 1615 to 1622; archbishop of Santiago de Compostela from 1622 to 1624; and archbishop of Seville in 1625, when he died.
[3] Marilyn Norcini, "The Political Process of Factionalism and Self-Governance at Santa Clara Pueblo, New Mexico," *Proceedings of the American Philosophical Society* 149.4 (2005), 544-590, ProQuest Central.
[4] Sarai Pérez Herrera, "Diego Fernández de Córdoba y el palacio del marquesado de Guadalcázar," *Tiempos Modernos*, 21 (February, 2010), accessed January 2, 2020, https://tinyurl.com/y6nor62g

year-old Margaret of Austria safely to Spain for her betrothal to twenty-one-year-old Philip III, thereby reinforcing the relationship between the two main branches of the Habsburg family. The journey was successful and the young couple married in Valencia on April 18, 1599.

Margaret's arrival at the Spanish royal palace in Madrid proved essential to Fernández's fortunes. Margaret became a significant political figure within the court. Having brought her own retinue to Spain, including her own confessor and ladies-in-waiting, she became an unofficial representative of the Austrian Habsburgs in Madrid and an important counterweight to Philip III's primary advisor, the Duke of Lerma.[5] Margaret also influenced Fernández's life in three significant ways. First, she introduced Fernández to her best friend, Maria Sidonia Riderer, who in turn helped pave the way for Fernández's marriage to Mariana Riderer Paar. This made Fernández the brother-in-law of Margaret's closest friend.[6] Second, Margaret probably facilitated Fernández's promotion to marquis in 1609, three years after the death of Fernández's father, the Lord of

Figure 1: "King of Spain Philip and Queen Margaret of Austria," print by Johann Ammon, 1648, Klebebände (Band 1), page 33, courtesy of Fürstlich Waldecksche Hofbibliothek and the University of Kassel, accessed October 2022, https://digi.ub.uni-heidelberg.de/fwhb/klebeband1

---

[5] Magdalena S. Sánchez, *The Empress, the Queen and the Nun: Women and Power at the Court of Philip III of Spain* (Baltimore, Maryland: 1998), 2-4, 21-22.
[6] Sánchez, *The Empress, the Queen and the Nun*, 29; and Pérez Herrera, "Diego Fernández de Córdoba y el palacio del marquesado de Guadalcázar."

Guadalcázar.[7] This noble rank allowed the new Marqués de Guadalcázar to win an honorary position in the royal household as gentlemen of the bedchamber, serving essentially as a chamberlain to the king.[8] This post gave Fernández coveted access to Philip III, a monarch who cherished his privacy.[9] In turn, this increased familiarity between the king and the Marqués de Guadalcázar facilitated Margaret's third and most important intervention on Fernández's behalf. Just before her death in childbirth, Margaret convinced Philip III to appoint Fernández the viceroy of New Spain[10] over other candidates whose bribes and backroom negotiations made the appointment difficult to obtain.[11] Fernández, then, owed both his family and his career to Margaret.

Fernández and Mariana arrived in Veracruz, Mexico in October 1612 after a voyage of about seventy-five-days[12] across the Atlantic and through the Caribbean. They were then two of the most important people in the New World. This status stemmed from both the viceroy's vast physical jurisdiction and the immense duties entrusted to him. Fernández formally governed what is today Mexico, Central America, most of the Caribbean, Venezuela, New Mexico, Florida, and the Philippines. He supervised the tax collection for the Crown, managed the treasury and the distribution of coinage, and enforced Spain's restrictive commercial policies. He appointed and removed officials from various offices, commanded troops, built military fortifications, modified royal orders, distributed land, guaranteed titles, founded new towns, oversaw hospitals and schools, maintained food stores for emergencies, and directed public projects like roads and aqueducts.[13] In addition, the viceroy had a responsibility for promoting Catholicism in his role as the primary propagator of the faith in the Spanish colonies. Fernández both not only authorized the construction and maintenance of all churches, convents and monasteries, but he also oversaw

---

[7] There was an "inflation of honors" during Philip III's reign. Fernández's elevation was one of thirty to the level of marquis; there were also three new dukes and thirty-three new counts in the Spanish nobility by 1630. See J. H. Elliott, *Imperial Spain 1469-1716* (New York: Penguin Books, 1990), 314.

[8] The official title in Spanish is *Gentilhombres de cámara con ejercicio*. See Pérez Herrera, "Diego Fernández de Córdoba y el palacio del marquesado de Guadalcázar."

[9] Sánchez, *The Empress, the Queen and the Nun*, 11.

[10] Sánchez, *The Empress, the Queen and the Nun*, 29.

[11] Hector Jaime Trevino Villarreal, "Diego Fernandez." *El Norte*, Mar 13, 1999, 8, ProQuest Central.

[12] Murdo J. Macleod, "Spain and America: The Atlantic Trade 1492-1700," *The Cambridge History of Latin America, Volume 1, Colonial Latin America*, Leslie Bethell (ed.) (New York, Cambridge University Press, 1984), 353.

[13] Lillian Estelle Fisher, *Viceregal Administration in the Spanish-American Colonies* (Berkeley, California: University of California Press, 1926), 2, 19, 58, 91-94, 129-130, 182, 251, 303.

Figure 2: Map of Latin America by Derek Dwight Anderson.

religious orders, held the archbishop and the diocesan clergy accountable, and had the final word on the appointment of all church offices within New Spain.[14] In short, the Marqués de Guadalcázar was the personification of the king in North America, which is why his arrival was met with elaborate welcoming ceremonies, including an inauguration day that drew upon the Roman tradition of an emperor's triumphal entrance into a city.[15] This too was great political theater.

---

[14] All of this was a function of Spain's unique relationship with the Papacy. In the papal bull *Eximiae devotionis* of *November 16, 1501*, Pope Alexander VI granted Spanish kings the right to collect tithes, build churches, and provide support for the clergy on the Papacy's behalf. In 1583, these powers were entrusted to the viceroy for New Spain. See Fisher, *Viceregal Administration in the Spanish-American Colonies*, 182-183, 186, 191,197, 215.

[15] Anna More, *Baroque Sovereignty: Carlos de Sigüenza y Góngora and the Creole Archive of Colonial Mexico* (Philadelphia, Pennsylvania, 2013), 111.

On October 28, 1612,[16] the colony's officialdom, dressed in their most fanciful and splendid attire, lined up and processed into Mexico City in a highly prescribed order: university professors and bureaucrats near the front, members of the city council (*cabildo*) and the city's chief magistrate (*corregidor*) in the middle, and the judges (*oidores*) of district-level judicial tribunals (*audiencias*) near the end.[17] At the rear of the procession, in the place of most importance, came the viceroy, shaded by a sixty-foot tawny canopy and riding a white horse with a black saddle, gold stirrups and gold bridal. He was dressed in gold-threaded garments so impressive that it seemed the sun itself rode the stallion.[18] The impact on the crowd would have been one of collective delight, jubilation, and awe.[19]

The procession's first destination was the Plaza of Santo Domingo, where a free-standing, ninety-foot triumphal arch had been constructed by the *cabildo* for the oath-taking ceremony. Decorated with paintings and statuary to evoke works from antiquity and emblazoned with poems and text, the arch's iconography honored the viceroy's position and challenged him to perform his duties faithfully.[20] Fernández then took his oath, received a symbolic key to the city, and walked through the arch as the city's ruler and defender. From the Plaza of Santo Domingo, the procession passed through the heart of the city to the main square and the cathedral, where the archbishop received Fernández and the canons sang *Te Deum laudamus*, an ancient hymn reserved for the most solemn occasions.[21] After high mass, Fernández and Mariana crossed the Zócalo, or main square, and as night fell, they entered the Baroque viceregal palace for the first time.[22] The financial costs of the day's events were high, but, in a society that equated displays of magnificence and expenditure with effective government, the day's

---

[16] Domingo Francisco de San Antón Muñón Chimalpahin Cuauhtlehuanitzin, *Annals of His Time: Don Domingo de San Antón Muñón Chimalpahin Quauhtlehuanitzin*, James Lockhart, Susan Schroeder, and Doris Namala (ed. and trans.) (Stanford, California: Stanford University Press, 2006), 231.

[17] Alejandro Cañeque, *The King's Living Image: The Culture and Politics of Viceregal Power in Colonial Mexico* (New York: Routledge, 2004), 123-124.

[18] This description is based on the procession in 1640 but is representative of the inaugural processions of other viceroys. See Linda A. Curcio-Nagy, *The Great Festivals of Colonial Mexico City: Performing Power and Identity* (Albuquerque, New Mexico: University of New Mexico Press, 2004), 16.

[19] Jacqueline Holler, "Of Sadness and Joy in Colonial Mexico," *Emotions and Daily Life in Colonial Mexico*, Javier Villa-Flores and Sonya Lipsett-Rivera (ed.) (Albuquerque, New Mexico: University of New Mexico Press, 2014), 36.

[20] Anna More, *Carlos de Sigüenza y Góngora and the Creole Archive of Colonial Mexico* (Philadelphia, Pennsylvania, 2013), 112.

[21] Cañeque, *The King's Living Image*, 124-125.

[22] Chimalpahin, *Annals of His Time*, 231.

ceremonies required grandeur.[23] Only in this way could the town leaders ensure that the community would pay homage as the *cabildo* gained the opportunity to buy influence.

Despite all this fanfare for the viceroy, there were significant limitations on his power. Many of these derived from the overlapping jurisdictions of the complex bureaucracy in the Spanish empire. On the political side, these counterbalances included district-level judicial tribunals called *audiencias*, which included judges (*oidores*) and crown attorneys (*fiscals*). What gave the *audiencia* real power in relation to the viceroys was its ability to communicate directly with royal officials in Madrid. In turn, members of the *audiencia* were held in check by local town councils (*cabildos*), who could appeal directly to the viceroy. Viceroys also typically had to face a visitor-general, an inspector sent directly by the king to audit both the viceroy and the *audiencia*. Thus every level of the bureaucracy had some built-in redundancy so that when disputes arose every institution had somewhere to appeal. It possessed a certain democratic sophistication, but it was not an efficient system. This was especially true because of the pervasive attitude at all levels of government that it was permissible to acknowledge rules without necessarily obeying them.[24] Reaching a final decision on any issue was almost impossible,[25] and Fernández swam in an ocean of paper as a result, corresponding with the various constituencies above and below him.

The political system's overlapping jurisdictions were further complicated by the state's unique relationship with the Church. The Spanish Church's autonomy from Rome meant no papal nuncio* was ever allowed to visit the New World to inspect Spanish churches, review church appointments, or evaluate its missionary efforts. The Church's dependence on the viceroy also meant frequent conflicts between bishops and viceroys over policy, status, and authority as the Church grew to thirty-four bishoprics and archbishoprics in the Spanish colonies by 1620.[26] The growth of religious orders in New Spain and the competitiveness between groups like the Franciscans, Dominicans, Augustinians, Carmelites, and Jesuits further complicated the situation. These groups fought with one another and the regular clergy over doctrinal issues central to the salvation of souls,

---

[23] Curcio-Nagy, *The Great Festivals of Colonial Mexico City*, 18. In September 1603, Viceroy Monterrey's eight-day reception for his successor, the Marqués de Montesclaros, cost Monterey a year's salary. See *The Works of Hubert Howe Bancroft, Volume XI, History of Mexico, Volume III, 1600-1803*, 5.

[24] J. H. Elliott, "Spain and America in the Sixteenth and Seventeenth Centuries," *The Cambridge History of Latin America, Volume 1, Colonial Latin America*, Leslie Bethell (ed.) (New York, Cambridge University Press, 1984), 303.

[25] Jeffery A. Cole, *The Potosí Mita, 1573-1700: Compulsive Labor in the Andes* (Stanford, California: Stanford University Press, 1985), 69.

[26] Elliott, "Spain and America in the Sixteenth and Seventeenth Centuries," 300-301.

mission territory, and the loyalty of the people. The orders opposed the establishment of one another's houses in certain cities, they tangled over their relative processional order in public ceremonies, and they quarreled about the use of devotional symbols. Each order also experienced internal turmoil over how strictly to adhere to their particular rules.[27] Two episodes during Fernández's term as viceroy provide excellent illustrations of the religious issues in New Spain in the seventeenth century.

The first involved a prominent and outspoken Jesuit preacher named Father Gómez. On August 13, 1618, Gómez criticized Fernández's sale of prestigious offices to Spaniards born in the Americas, or Creoles. The practice of selling offices was not in and of itself controversial or new. In fact, in an effort to increase revenues, Philip II began selling offices in 1591. Fifteen years later, Philip III amplified the practice, as well as the problem, by allowing current office holders to sell their own positions if the Crown received in taxes one third to one half of the purchase price.[28] Gómez, however, argued that the sale of offices to Creoles threatened the established privileges of the *Peninsulares*, who he argued were by definition more competent administrators than those born in the Americas.[29] In his utter denigration of the Creoles, Gómez asserted that they were incapable of running anything, even a hen pen, let alone a city or a district.[30] In reality, though, the Creoles were often wealthier than the appointees from Spain.

These statements inflamed Gómez's largely Creole audience at the chapel of the San Hipólito hospital that August morning. By the end of the second decade of the seventeenth century, Creoles were deeply involved in creating their own sense of identity: they were on the verge of using the term "criollo" with a sense of pride and ownership.[31] Gómez's audience responded to his denigration by drawing their swords, ending the mass in turmoil and acrimony, and calling for Gómez's censure. Archbishop Pérez de la Serna responded to the situation by revoking Gómez's license to preach, but this produced Jesuit indignation since

---

[27] Karen Melvin, *Building Colonial Cities of God: Mendicant Orders and Urban Culture* (Stanford, California: Stanford University Press, 2012), 10, 144, 187, 194.
[28] Louisa Schell Hoberman, *Mexico's Merchant Elite, 1590-1660: Silver, State and Society* (Durham, North Carolina, Duke University Press, 1991), 11. Hoberman also notes that this practice generally diminished the quality of office holders over time.
[29] Interestingly, these tensions between *Peninsulares* and Creoles also occurred within the mendicant orders themselves, where by 1610 Creoles dominated the membership of both the Dominicans and the Augustinians. The Franciscans also had a large number of Creoles and experienced significant bitterness between those who were Spanish-born and those who were not. See J.I. Israel, *Race, Class and Politics in Colonial Mexico, 1610-1670* (London: Oxford University Press, 1975), 103.
[30] Israel, *Race, Class and Politics in Colonial Mexico, 1610-1670*, 85.
[31] More, *Baroque Sovereignty*, 8-12.

archbishops have no authority over the members of the Jesuit order. The controversy simmered for a month with the archbishop ordering each church in the city to give a sermon praising Creoles on September 20, while the Jesuits stood by Gómez and brought in a special counsel to defend him. The archbishop upped the ante by arresting this counsel, while the Jesuits, in turn, appealed to Fernández for assistance. The viceroy, who had no personal affection for the archbishop, sided with the Jesuits, and with the cooperation of the *audiencia*, successfully freed the special counsel from the archbishop's jail. Thus the viceroyalty's most prominent authorities were at loggerheads, each working to undermine every other, but all knew that this much open conflict threatened the established order. A face-saving compromise had to be found in order to preserve the legitimacy of the archbishop, the Jesuits, Gómez, the special counsel, and Fernández. In the end, the viceroy brokered an agreement. It allowed Gómez to deliver the official Jesuit New Year's sermon for 1619, but then required him to leave the city for many months.[32] This compromise restored the appearance of harmony between colonial leaders.

Another example from Fernández's term that illustrates the overlapping jurisdictions and rivalries in early seventeenth century New Spain involved the doctrine of Immaculate Conception. Early Christian and medieval theologians had long wrestled with the quandary of the Virgin Mary and original sin: How was it possible for Mary to be both conceived by human parents and free of original sin? By the

Figure 3: "Diego Fernández de Córdoba, 1st Marquess of Guadalcázar," painting by unknown artist, unknown date, courtesy of Museo Nacional de Historia (MNH), Mexico City and Wikimedia Commons.

---

[32] Israel, *Race, Class and Politics in Colonial Mexico, 1610-1670*, 84-86.

seventeenth century, the twelve-hundred-year-old debate had coalesced into two camps: one led by the Dominicans, who followed the scholastic* tradition and Thomas Aquinas; and one led by Franciscans, who followed Duns Scotus and the humanist tradition. The Dominicans argued that only Christ was free of original sin because only Christ was conceived without sexual intercourse. Having human parents, Mary could not have been conceived without original sin, and she too needed Christ's power of salvation.[33] To claim otherwise was to deny Christ's power as the universal redeemer, and that was an untenable proposition for any Christian. Conversely, the Franciscans emphasized the corruption of the soul instead of the body through sexual intercourse, thereby breaking the connection between the body, procreation, and original sin posited by St. Augustine. For the Franciscans, God made Mary free of sin at the moment of her conception, providing the greatest example of Christ's power to save souls.[34]

Philip III endorsed the Franciscan position in 1616 and the first large-scale, public celebration of the Immaculate Conception occurred in New Spain two years later. As part of the preparations for the event, the silversmith's guild* in Mexico City constructed a four-foot statue of the Virgin Mary in pure silver. They also made blue cloaks emblazoned with the words, "Mary conceived without original sin" in silver. On the feast day, Fernández, the *audiencia*, Archbishop Juan Pérez de la Serna, his clergy, and the members of the male mendicant orders processed through the streets and triumphal arches to collect the statue and bring it to the cathedral. Along the way, the procession stopped at the Franciscans' primary church, where congratulatory fireworks were set off, and at a Franciscan nunnery, where the nuns greeted the parade with music. Once in the cathedral, the silver statue and the concept of Immaculate Conception were then celebrated continuously for the next week as large crowds venerated the new statue.[35]

The Dominicans did not accept Philip III's endorsement of the doctrine and responded to the public celebration by writing sonnets poking fun at the members of the other orders. The sonnets ridiculed Franciscans for their spurious theology, the Augustinians for their problematic humanism, the Carmelites for their excessive wealth, and the Jesuits for preaching little of value. Not to be outdone as poets, representatives of these now-abused orders then wrote sonnets of their own and distributed them to artisans and merchants

---

[33] Sarah Jane Boss, "The Development of the Doctrine of Mary's Immaculate Conception," *Mary: The Complete Resource*, Sarah Jane Boss (ed.) (New York: Continuum, 2007), 212.
[34] Boss, "The Development of the Doctrine of Mary's Immaculate Conception," 208-209, 212-214.
[35] Melvin, *Building Colonial Cities of God*, 207, 210.

throughout Mexico City.[36] This spurred considerable conversation and debate between laypeople and clergy alike, but the Dominicans' efforts to discredit their fellow clerics and to decide the theological question did not work. In 1662, the news reached Mexico that the pope had prohibited anyone from saying that Mary had been conceived with sin and had ordered the Inquisition to investigate anyone who said she had been.[37]

Philip II established the Holy Office of the Inquisition in the Americas in 1569 to protect the Catholic faith "in all the purity and completeness necessary" so that the New World might be "free from errors and false and suspicious doctrines." The pious king also ordered that all officials in the viceroyalties of New Spain and Peru cooperate with the inquisitors "with due and decent reverence and respect," aiding the Holy Office "whenever it is requested...in order to arrest whatever heretics or suspects in faith they may find."[38] The Inquisition's purpose was to identify and root out heresy, blasphemy, adultery, bigamy, witchcraft, idolatry, and homosexuality among the people and immorality within the clergy. All of these behaviors represented perceived threats to the social order. By censoring books and other printed works and by investigating suspicious individuals and bringing them to trial, the Inquisition acted as the colonies' moral disciplinarian.[39] During Fernández's term as viceroy, for example, the Holy Office issued an edict in 1616 that ordered the population to denounce practitioners of astrology and other forms of divination and to surrender all books relating to such practices. It also prohibited the use of peyote in 1620, describing its hallucinogenic effects as "vile illusions" triggered by the devil in order to "trick the simple minds" of Indians who possess "a natural inclination towards idolatry."[40] And it

---

[36] Melvin, *Building Colonial Cities of God*, 208-209.

[37] Melvin, *Building Colonial Cities of God*, 212. Since the Spanish Inquisition was independent of the Inquisition elsewhere, this edict would not have technically applied to New Spain, but the effect was pronounced nonetheless. In 1854, Pope Pius IV issued a papal bull finalizing the Church's position in favor of Franciscan viewpoint. See Pius IX, "*Ineffabilis Deus*: The Immaculate Conception," *Papal Encyclicals Online*, accessed January 2, 2020 https://www.papalencyclicals.net/pius09/p9ineff.htm

[38] "Royal Order Issued by King Philip II Establishing the Foundation of the Holy Office of the Inquisition in the Indies," *The Inquisition in New Spain, 1536-1820: A Documentary History*, John F. Chuchiak IV (ed. and trans.) (Baltimore, Maryland: The Johns Hopkins University Press, 2012), 81-82.

[39] C.H. Haring, *The Spanish Empire in America* (New York: Harbinger Books, 1963), 189.

[40] "Edict of Faith that Requires All to Denounce the Practitioners of Astrology, Necromancy, Geomancy..." and "Edict of Faith Concerning the Illicit Use of Peyote," in *The Inquisition in New Spain, 1536-1820*, 110-114.

reprimanded a parish priest in 1614 for stepping far beyond his authority in illegally conducting trials and punishments of the indigenous population.[41]

Despite its reputation for vitriolic and sadistic judges who quickly handed down pre-determined verdicts, the Inquisition was a complex bureaucracy with a well-defined legal process.[42] This process involved a preliminary investigation and required collaborating eyewitness testimony, proof without *any* doubt (as opposed to proof beyond a reasonable doubt), and a review by a council that examined the transcripts and verdicts before sentencing. Throughout the process, the Inquisition protected witnesses by granting them complete anonymity. It could use torture to obtain information and confessions, but defendants had to reaffirm their statements while not being tortured in order for these statements to have validity.[43] At the conclusion of a trial, the Holy Office regularly showcased its authority and its teachings during a public ceremony, an *auto-de-fé*, in which the convicted publicly performed a penance. For the most egregious offenses, usually involving individuals who refused to recant or were repeat offenders, the Inquisition ordered the guilty to be burned alive.

Unfortunately for Philip II and those who fervently desired to establish a kingdom of God in the Americas, by the early seventeenth century the Inquisition was less ferocious and omnipresent in New Spain than its reputation today would suggest. Between 1571-1700, the Holy Office held 1,913 trials in New Spain: 29.7% involving minor religious crimes, 27.5% dealing with formal heresy, 24.1% entailing sexual crimes, and 7.2% comprising witchcraft. Significantly, these 1,913 cases represented just 5% of those tried in peninsular Spain.[44] Even more tellingly, the punishments meted out were more lenient than in Spain itself. In New Spain, the death penalty was only used in 1% of the cases. The second highest level of punishment (a loss of property, public flogging, imprisonment followed by forced labor) occurred in 18.3% of the cases, as opposed to 70% of the cases in peninsular Spain. Taken together, these statistics show how much less intense the Inquisition was in the Americas than in Spain itself. In short, the Inquisition was not a daily concern for most of those under Fernández's

---

[41] J. Richard Andrews and Ross Hassig, "Editor's Introduction," *Treatise on the Heathen Superstitions that Live Among the Indians Native to this New Spain* (Norman, Oklahoma: University of Oklahoma Press, 1987), 7.

[42] Irene Silverblatt, *Modern Inquisitions: Peru and the Colonial Origins of the Civilized World* (Durham, North Carolina: Duke University Press, 2004), 5-7.

[43] John F. Chuchiak IV, "The Holy Office of the Inquisition in New Spain (Mexico): An Introductory Study," *The Inquisition in New Spain, 1536-1820*, 33-45.

[44] Chuchiak, "The Holy Office of the Inquisition in New Spain (Mexico)," 7. The remaining 11.5% involved solicitation, civil crimes, and idolatry. Formal heresy involved things like practicing Judaism, Islam, or Protestantism or professing schismatic propositions or false mysticism.

jurisdiction, even if those in Mexico City felt the Inquisition's presence more than those in other parts of New Spain.[45]

One of the reasons for this decreased emphasis centered upon the attitude of government officials. The Holy Office was as an arm of the state rather than the Church, so the Holy Office's mission required active cooperation between the viceroy and the inquisitors. Government officials, however, frequently boycotted required Holy Office events. Even numerous viceroys failed to attend occasions that the Holy Office saw as essential.[46] Fernández seems to have been one of the officials with a rather lackadaisical attitude about the Inquisition's mission. Between 1610-1619, only 83 cases came before New Spain's inquisitors. The majority of these involved bigamy (22), blasphemy (9) and witchcraft (5), and there were only two cases about heresy.[47] Even more tellingly, no *auto-de-fé* was held during Fernández's term as viceroy.[48]

Another reason for the limited success of the Inquisition in seventeenth century Mexico was that the Holy Office frequently came into conflict with members of the diocesan clergy and officials in the Church hierarchy, who once had the responsibilities now given to the Inquisition.[49] Rivalry and jealousy over moral authority also hampered the Inquisition. With key institutional and societal leaders only marginally supporting the Holy Office, its unpopularity spread to the general population. People refused to surrender their banned books, and individuals even openly ridiculed Inquisition judges. In 1615, for example, one woman in Mexico City publicly described the inquisitors as "nothing but a bunch of drunks and fools who do not know what they are doing."[50]

Nonetheless, the Inquisition pursued certain cases with particular assiduousness. Frequently these cases involved Jews.

---

[45] Chuchiak, "The Holy Office of the Inquisition in New Spain (Mexico), xv, 48.
[46] Martin Austin Nesvig, *Ideology and Inquisition: The World of the Censors in Early Mexico* (New Haven, Connecticut: Yale University Press, 2009), 191.
[47] Nesvig, *Ideology and Inquisition*, 171.
[48] Elkan Nathan Adler, *Auto de Fé and Jew* (London: Oxford University Press, 1908), 154. Adler does list one *auto-de-fé* occurring in 1621, but does not give the specific date. It is very unlikely that this occurred before Fernández left Mexico for Peru in March 1621, especially given the nature of Fernández's departure detailed below.
[49] Elliott, "Spain and America in the Sixteenth and Seventeenth Centuries," 302.
[50] Ana de Aranda quoted in Martin Austin Nesvig, *Ideology and Inquisition: The World of the Censors in Early Mexico* (New Haven, Connecticut: Yale University Press, 2009), 191. Ana de Aranda was not punished for these words even if the Holy Office found them to be "scandalous and offensive to pious ears."

~

Judaism is arguably the oldest of the world's monotheistic religions, but the method by which Jews honored God's singularity changed irrevocably in 70 CE, when the Romans destroyed the Temple in Jerusalem and expelled the Jews from the city. No longer able to perform ritual animal sacrifices in their only House of God, Jews had to create a new liturgical tradition. They became the People of the Book. They studied the Torah (the first five books of the Hebrew Bible) and the Talmud (the rabbinical commentary which forms the basis of Jewish law) and came to believe that studying was the proper way to understand God, rather than performing animal sacrifices. Not everything about Judaism changed, however. Jews continued to profess that God is not a physical being but an essence that is all-powerful and all-knowing. Many also maintained their belief that upon death humans are judged by Him, and many continued to trust that God will vindicate his Chosen People by one day creating a perfect society on Earth.

Jews migrated to the Iberian peninsula as early as the third century. They flourished in the early years of Islamic Spain in the eighth century, as Muslims frequently left Jews in charge of managing the towns they had conquered.[51] Through the course of the Middle Ages, however, tensions came to mark the interactions between Jews, Muslims, and Christians, even as all three communities also interacted regularly as a result of commercial, scientific, or other professional reasons.[52] There were particularly vicious persecutions of Jews in Spain in 1391 and 1449. Then in 1492, Christian forces captured Granada, and the victorious Spanish monarchs, King Ferdinand and Queen Isabella, ordered the expulsion of all Jews from Spain in an effort to create a purely Christian kingdom. Some Jews, called *conversos*, converted to Christianity rather than leave Spain.[53] Others departed for Islamic North Africa, and as many as 100,000 migrated to Portugal, where they were able to purchase admission to the country. Just five years later, however, the Portuguese king, Manuel I, began forcing Christian baptism upon Jews, perhaps to improve his chances of marrying

---

[51] Chris Lowney, *A Vanished World: Muslims, Christians, and Jews in Medieval Spain* (New York: Oxford University Press, 2006), 96.
[52] Joseph Pérez, *History of a Tragedy: The Expulsion of the Jews from Spain*, Lysa Hochroth (trans.) (Urbana, Illinois: University of Illinois Press, 2007), 8-18.
[53] *Conversos* were also known as "New Christians," but many were thought to be crypto-Jews, who had not truly accepted the Catholic faith and who continued to practice Judaism in private. This led long-standing Christian Spaniards to pass blood purity laws ("Limpieza de sangre"), forcing people to prove their multi-generational Christian ancestry as a test of the sincerity of faith.

Ferdinand and Isabella's daughter.[54] This created more *conversos*, many of whom continued to practice Judaism in secret. Others hid their identities and migrated to the Americas, despite repeated Spanish royal decrees in the sixteenth century that prohibited Jews from entering the New World.[55] During the first decade of the seventeenth century, however, the situation changed when Philip III began allowing open migration to his colonies. The number of descendants of *conversos* moving to the Americas grew considerably between 1601 and 1609 as a result. So many Jews, crypto-Jews, and former Jews came from Portugal to New Spain that Inquisition records use the words for "Jews" and "Portuguese" as virtual synonyms.

Once in the viceroyalty of New Spain, most Jews became shopkeepers, peddlers, and craftsmen, but the wealthiest members of the Jewish community were members of the commercial elite, specializing in the trade of slaves, cacao, and textiles.[56] Jews in places like Mexico City usually had to appear to be proper Christians in public. They had to be creative in the ways they hid their Judaism, from being less literal about kosher dietary laws, feigning illness to avoid working during the Sabbath, creating synagogues in private homes, and using a modified, longitudinal circumcision in the teenage years instead of at birth.[57] They had little knowledge of Hebrew, but knew the basic tenets of Jewish law.[58] Over time, New Spain's Jews also incorporated elements of Catholicism into their rituals, such as praying with outstretched arms, believing in purgatory,* and employing the intervention of saints.[59] But Judaism survived: according to mid-sixteenth century records, Jews comprised 22% of Mexico City's White[60] population during the first half of the seventeenth century, and *conversos* controlled at least 20% of

---

[54] François Soyer, *The Persecution of the Jews and Muslims in Portugal: King Manuel I and the End of Religious Tolerance* (Leiden, The Netherlands: Brill NV, 2007), 177.

[55] When Spain's Philip II became King of Portugal in 1580 as a result of a dynastic struggle in Portugal, many *conversos* temporarily returned to Spain and then migrated to the Spanish colonies in the Americas. The crowns remained united until 1640.

[56] Israel, *Race, Class and Politics in Colonial Mexico, 1610-1670*, 128.

[57] Seymour B. Liebman, *The Jews in New Spain: Faith, Flame and the Inquisition* (Coral Gables, Florida: University of Miami Press, 1970), 57, 64, 71-72, 76-77.

[58] Israel, *Race, Class and Politics in Colonial Mexico, 1610-1670*, 129.

[59] Liebman, *The Jews in New Spain*, 72.

[60] In the wake of the protests following George Floyd's death in Minneapolis, Minnesota on May 25, 2020, the National Association of Black Journalists (NABJ) released the following statement: "it is important to capitalize 'Black' when referring to (and out of respect for) the Black diaspora. NABJ also recommends that whenever a color is used to appropriately describe race then it should be capitalized, including White and Brown." I have adopted this style recommendation as a result, except when quoting from a primary source. See National Association of Black Journalists, "NABJ Statement on Capitalizing Black and Other Racial Identifiers," June 2020, accessed August 27, 2020, https://www.nabj.org/page/styleguide

Figure 4: "Four Views of Mexico City," print by unknown artist, c.1680 – 1725, courtesy of Rijksmuseum, Amsterdam, RP-P-1910-4056-4.

New Spain's Atlantic trade. Jews, however private about their religious practices, played an important role in Mexico City, Puebla, and other major communities in New Spain.[61]

The Inquisition in New Spain pursued cases against Jews erratically, but the periods of persecution tended to be intense. The worst came between 1590 and 1600 and between 1640 and 1650. At an *auto-de-fé* on April 11, 1649 in Mexico City, for example, 65 Jews were burnt in effigy, 9 were banished, 19 reconciled, 12 whipped to death and then burnt, and one was burnt alive.[62] Not all cases ended up in convictions, however. In 1615, for example, a learned man in the town of Zacatecas was accused by multiple witnesses of being a Jew; he questioned Jesus' standing as the Messiah as a result of Jesus being the son of a carpenter and being crucified. The man denied in court the interpretation these witnesses ascribed to his words and was apparently set free since the Holy Office never arrested him or sequestered his property.[63] Overall, cases against Jews between 1571 and 1700 formed 6.8% of the total cases tried by the Holy Office.[64]

~

---

[61] Liebman, *The Jews in New Spain*, 21, 42.
[62] Elkan Nathan Adler, *Auto de Fé and Jew* (London: Oxford University Press, 1908), 155.
[63] Liebman, *The Jews in New Spain*, 74, 208.
[64] "Trials and Testimonies Against Jewish and Crypto-Jewish Practices," *The Inquisition in New Spain, 1536-1820: A Documentary History*, John F. Chuchiak IV (ed. and trans.) (Baltimore, Maryland: The Johns Hopkins University Press, 2012), 235-236.

Diego Fernández de Córdoba, the Marqués de Guadalcázar, faced a number of other challenges during his eight-and-a-half years as viceroy of New Spain. Some of these were perennial, faced by every viceroy; others were particular to Fernández's term. In the eyes of the Mexico City wealthiest, the most important issue for any viceroy was to manage involved commercial activity. Consequently, one of the first groups to seek an audience with the Marqués de Guadalcázar was the merchant community's elite.

By the second decade of the seventeenth century, Mexico City was an emporium of the world's merchandise because Spain was near the zenith of its economic influence, connecting Asian, American, and European goods as its galleons plied the Atlantic and the Pacific Oceans.[65] Mexico City's markets filled with European clocks, Chinese silks, Persian rugs, Japanese screens, Indonesian spices, Cambodian ivory, Angolan slaves, Guatemalan cacao, and Peruvian wine.[66] While 50% of all shipping between Spain and the New World passed through Mexico during this period, the Pacific trade was of even greater concern for the city's elite merchants since only they possessed the resources to handle the high costs incumbent in trading between Acapulco and Manila.[67] In fact, between 1610 and 1619, just seventeen men controlled 94% of the Pacific trade, and the vast majority of them were Spanish-born.[68] These men petitioned Fernández repeatedly to expand trade in the Pacific and to reduce the number of regulations governing it. These merchants pointed out that when the Mexico-Philippine trade began in 1567 no regulations existed. The free market determined both the goods exchanged and their prices. This made it more attractive for New Spain's merchants to obtain goods from Asia than from Spain. In fact, by 1597 the amount of Mexican silver leaving Acapulco for the Philippines exceeded the value of all Mexican trade to Spain.[69] Royal officials in Madrid, however, were mercantilists,* who believed that colonies existed for the benefit of the mother country, and that the economy had to be controlled to be effective and prosperous. These officials also believed that the Pacific trade should further Spanish political and religious goals in Asia, which ranged from limiting Dutch expansion to supporting a base from which Christianity might be brought to China. Consequently, Philip II began imposing regulations on the Pacific trade in 1582. In an effort to prevent the drainage of South American silver to Asia, he

---

[65] Israel, *Race, Class and Politics in Colonial Mexico, 1610-1670*, 21.
[66] Rainer F. Buschmann, Edward R. Slack, Jr., and James B. Tueller, *Navigating the Spanish Lake: The Pacific in the Iberian World, 1521-1898* (Honolulu, Hawai'i: University of Hawai'i Press, 2013) 26.
[67] Hoberman, *Mexico's Merchant Elite, 1590-1660*, 32.
[68] Hoberman, *Mexico's Merchant Elite, 1590-1660*, 39, 41.
[69] Elliott, "Spain and America in the Sixteenth and Seventeenth Centuries," 325.

also imposed regulations on the trade between New Spain and Peru. By 1604, royal regulations held that only three galleons of no more than 400 tons could sail between Acapulco and Lima, and these ships were expressly forbidden to carry Asian goods.[70] The merchants meeting with Fernández found these rules far too constraining and pointed out that demand for Asian goods far outstripped what three ships per year could carry. They repeatedly urged the viceroy to change the regulations so that honorable merchants could remain in accordance with the law and help the Crown fight piracy. Fernández, however, could not convince Spanish court officials to allow more trade, so the problem of illegal trading worsened. By 1618, the estimated value of illegal trade between Acapulco and the Philippines was at least 100% of the value of the legal trade.[71]

One reason Fernández made such little headway regarding royal economic policies was that Spanish manufacturers were angry about the competition from colonial manufactured goods. They complained that their exports had fallen since the peak in 1608.[72] One reason for the decline was that by the seventeenth century New Spain didn't need Spanish goods as much as it had in the sixteenth. Because Spanish wine and oil could not arrive in Peru or Chile before it turned to vinegar or became rancid, these areas developed their own production. Similarly, in the textile industry it became easier and cheaper to produce cloth and clothing locally than to import these items from Spain. By 1604, therefore, Mexico City had 25 textile mills and ten hat factories.[73] In Peru, Europeans used local cloth to supplement their fashions.[74] As the colonies became increasingly independent economically, the balance of power between Spain and New Spain shifted.[75] Significantly, Fernández understood these changes, bragged about an increase in production of textiles from Puebla in 1612, and concluded that this revealed the colony's strength.[76] Since this ran quite contrary to their goals, officials in Spain were not impressed with this news. Their frustration only grew as the century progressed, for as the colonies developed their own illicit trade within the

---

[70] Hoberman, *Mexico's Merchant Elite, 1590-1660*, 214-216. Madrid's mercantilist fervor only grew over time as it tried to squeeze revenues out of the colonies in the Americas. In 1631, the Crown banned all direct trade between Peru and Mexico to direct as much silver as possible to Spain.
[71] Hoberman, *Mexico's Merchant Elite, 1590-1660*, 220.
[72] Macleod, "Spain and America," 370. This was the peak in both volume and variety.
[73] Israel, *Race, Class and Politics in Colonial Mexico, 1610-1670*, 20.
[74] Karen B. Graubart, *With Our Labor and Sweat: Indigenous Women and the Formation of Colonial Society in Peru, 1550-1700* (Stanford, California: Stanford University Press, 2007), 155.
[75] John Lynch, *Spain Under the Habsburgs, Volume II: Spain and America, 1598-1700* (New York: Oxford University Press, 1969), 13.
[76] Hoberman, *Mexico's Merchant Elite, 1590-1660*, 271.

Americas, Spain experienced a sharp decrease in both the number of arriving ships and the tonnage of the cargo.[77]

One of the best illustrations of the complexities of Spanish commerce can be seen in the various attempts to establish trade with Japan. Upon the urging of Franciscan missionaries in Japan, the Japanese sent their first envoys to Mexico in 1610 during the viceroyalty of Fernández's predecessor.[78] In response to this contact, the viceroy authorized explorer Sebastian Vizcaino to sail to Japan in March 1611 with six barefoot Franciscans, establish commercial relations with the Japanese, and spend time learning about the Japanese archipelago and its customs. This effort was partially thwarted by the Dutch, who convinced many Japanese officials that the Spanish were more interested in missionary activity than trade.[79] But Japanese lord Date Masamune was very keen to generate more diplomatic and commercial relations with the West and so made arrangements for one of his vassals, Hasekura Tsunenaga, to travel to Madrid and to Rome. The

Figure 5: "Portrait of Hasekura Tsunenaga," print by Raphael Sadeler, 1615, courtesy of Rijksmuseum, Amsterdam, RP-P-OB-7617.

---

[77] Geoffrey Parker, Global Crisis: *War, Climate Change, and Catastrophe in the Seventeenth Century* (New Haven, Connecticut: Yale University Press, 2013), 466-468. In fact, by 1650, the quantity of goods transported from the Americas to Spain had fallen to less than half the volume of 1600. Parker notes that the diversification of the economy and the retention of wealth in the Americas allowed the region to avoid the worst effects of climatic challenges caused by the seventeenth century's Little Ice Age and "General Crisis."

[78] The viceroy of New Spain from July 2, 1607 to June 19, 1611 was Luís de Velasco, Marquess of Salinas (1534-1617). The Japanese delegation did not have to go all the way to Madrid since, as the king's representative, the viceroy could negotiate on his behalf.

[79] *The Works of Hubert Howe Bancroft, Volume XI, History of Mexico, Volume III, 1600-1803*, 3-4.

San Juan Bautista sailed from Japan in October 1613 with 180 men on board, including its captain Vizcaino and a sixty-member Japanese embassy led by Hasekura.[80] The voyage to Mexico took the Spanish three months as a result of several debilitating storms, but they reached Acapulco in January 1614, and were greeted by a warm welcome with horns and drums booming. Upon the ship's arrival, the crew had their weapons confiscated, lest they might misbehave in a new land, but the Japanese seemed pleased with their reception.[81]

This auspicious beginning suffered a significant blow, however, when a Japanese officer beat and stabbed Captain Vizcaino for trying to take possession of the gifts the Japanese intended for Fernández, King Philip III, and Pope Paul V. Apparently the captain believed he deserved a reward for delivering the Japanese safely and with none forthcoming, he took matters into his own hands. The Japanese saw Vizcaino's attempted theft as a dishonorable act and acted accordingly, thereby illustrating the differences in cultural expectations that make trade and diplomacy so delicate. The Japanese worried about the impression the arrival of a bloodied Spanish captain would make and so sent an advance party to Mexico City. This contingent marched into the capital at twelve noon on March 4 with the soldiers dressed in "something like a tunic," their hair tied "at the back of their necks," and carrying "long, narrow, black poles, maybe their lances" in the lead, according to one eyewitness. The officers proudly followed on horseback.[82] By the time Hasekura and most of the rest of the delegation arrived on March 24, having taken a leisurely journey across the mountains from the coast, Vizcaino had had a chance to tell his side of the story but to little avail. Fernández saw to it that Hasekura and his officers were properly accommodated at a house near the San Francisco Monastery and the

---

[80] Thomas Christensen, *1616: The World in Motion* (Berkeley, California: Counterpoint, 2012), 330
[81] Takashi Gonoi, *Hasekura Tsunenaga* (Tokyo, Japan: Yoshikawa Kobunkan, 2003), 77. I am indebted to Takako and Hideko Akashi for their assistance in translating passages from this work into English for me.
[82] Chimalpahin, *Annals of His Time*, 273, 275. During the visit in 1610, Chimalpahin's journal entries describe the Japanese as a "bold, not gentle and meek people, going about like eagles." (171), and yet he is also surprised by their having beardless "faces like women…whitish and light" (173). Chimalpahin also comments at length on the hair of the men: "Their hair begins at their temples, all going around towards the nape of their necks. They are long-haired…[and] look like girls because of the way they wear their hair…[which] they tie in twisted, intertwined fashion, reaching to the middle of the head with close shaving. It really looks like a tonsure that they display on their heads." (171). Significantly, however, Chimalpahin's entries in 1614 do not dwell on these physical details; the Japanese have become far more known and far less foreign to him by then.

dispute with Vizcaino was forgotten.[83] Of greater concern to Fernández were those members of the New Spain business community who feared that trade with Japan would adversely affect the established trade with the Philippines. Fernández had to weigh these fears, while making sure that his Japanese guests were not offended by hostility they received from some quarters.[84] Such was the life of a viceroy: forever balancing various constituencies with contrasting needs and agendas, while maintaining proper diplomatic decorum and viceregal dignity. Since forty-two members of the Japanese delegation were baptized as Catholics in Mexico City in April 1614,[85] and since the majority of the delegation peacefully remained in Mexico City while Hasekura proceeded to Europe with twenty men, it is clear that Fernández proved able to establish an equilibrium.[86] He did, however, write to the Council of the Indies on October 30, 1614, questioning the wisdom of developing trade relations with the Japanese, given how poorly defended Spain's holdings on the Pacific coast were.[87]

A second major issue Fernández dealt with in his tenure as viceroy of New Spain was the flooding caused by the unusual topography surrounding the viceregal capital. Because it sat in a basin with no outlet for runoff water, excess precipitation drained into a shallow lake which covered about 19% of the valley

---

[83] According to Chimalpahin, during the Japanese visit in 1610 the viceroy sent his personal carriage to pick up the delegation's leader. Chimalpahin also briefly mentions a formal reception and meal at the viceroy's palace. By 1614, such accommodations did not deserve mention in his mind; it was a given. See Chimalpahin, 173, 275-276.

[84] Gonoi, *Hasekura Tsunenaga*, 87, 93. A more recent source notes that Fernández issued a specific order to maintain the peace in spite of the Japanese presence. He charged Dr. Antonio de Morga with the job of ensuring that the Japanese right to sell their merchandise was not infringed upon by other businessmen or the public. See Cornelius Conover, *Pious Imperialism: Spanish Rule and the Cult of the Saints in Mexico City* (Albuquerque, New Mexico: University of New Mexico Press, 2019), 50, 204.

[85] Chimalpahin, *Annals of His Time*, 277, 279.

[86] Hasekura did meet with King Philip III and Pope Paul V in 1614, but his embassy did not produce meaningful results. He returned to Mexico, traveled to the Philippines, and returned to Japan in 1620. Just after Hasekura departed Japan in 1613, Shogun Tokugawa Ieyasu expelled most Christians from Japan, making his mission impossible to fulfill. I have not been able to find any account of Fernández's impressions of the Japanese arrival or departure, either in 1614 or 1616. For more information about the event and its significance see Inaga Shigemi, "Japanese Encounters with Latin America and Iberian Catholicism (1549-1973): Some Thoughts on Language, Imperialism, Identity Formation, and Comparative Research." *The Comparatist* 32, (May, 2008): 27-35, ProQuest Central.

[87] Cornelius Conover, *Pious Imperialism: Spanish Rule and the Cult of the Saints in Mexico City* (Albuquerque, New Mexico: University of New Mexico Press, 2019), 204.

floor.[88] The Aztecs subdivided this lake with causeways, constructed floodgates, built floating gardens, and rerouted rivers in a successful effort to control flooding during the rainy season; their work also segregated brackish water, and increased food production in the area.[89] During the early colonial period, the Spanish failed to appreciate the complexity of the region's hydrology. Combined with increased soil erosion and little maintenance of Aztec water containment systems, this ignorance set the stage for significant problems.[90] In 1551, 1580, and 1604 the capital experienced substantial flooding and each attempt to correct the problem failed.[91] When another flood hit the city in 1607, the viceroy, Luís de Valesco, argued that the existing systems were "not strong or effective enough to assure this city's safety and perpetuity."[92] He convinced local elites to agree to a solution originally proposed five centuries earlier: drain the lakes out of the Valley of Mexico by constructing a drainage tunnel that led to rivers flowing to the Pacific Ocean. Funded by a tax on every slaughtered animal in the city, a tax on wine, and a one-time property assessment of 1.5%, and built with compulsory indigenous labor, the drainage project represented a massive undertaking. It required the construction of a fifteen-mile-long diversion dam, a four-mile-long trench, and a four-mile-long tunnel, which was eight feet wide and nine feet tall at the point of its greatest volume.[93] All this work and more took just ten months, due to the efforts of 60,000 Indian laborers. On September 17, 1608 water flowed out of the Valley of Mexico for the first time.[94]

By the time of Fernández's inauguration in December 1612, serious problems had crept into the project. The tunnel was too small to handle the required volume of water and the tunnel's slope was too steep; this eroded the tunnel's

---

[88] Vera S. Candiani, *Dreaming of Dry Land: Environmental Transformation in Colonial Mexico City* (Stanford, California: Stanford University Press, 2014), 16.

[89] Ivonne Del Valle, "On Shaky Ground: Hydraulics, State Formation and Colonialism in Sixteenth Century Mexico," *Hispanic Review*, 77.2 (Spring 2009), 197-220, ProQuest Central.

[90] Candiani, *Dreaming of Dry Land*, 28-29.

[91] By the seventeenth century, the one lake separated by causeways was no more. Instead, a series of separate lakes existed in the valley. The main, central lake, Texcoco, was closest to the capital city, had the lowest elevation, and was brackish. To the south stood the freshwater lakes of Chalco and Xochimilco, which were about five feet higher in elevation than Texcoco. To the north stood the freshwater lakes of Cristóbal and Zumpango, which were about ten feet and twenty-seven feet higher than Texcoco respectively. In the rainy season, Zumpango's overflow ran into Cristóbal, Cristóbal's overflow ran into Texcoco, and the city flooded. See *The Works of Hubert Howe Bancroft, Volume XI, History of Mexico, Volume III, 1600-1803*, 8.

[92] Luís de Valesco quoted in Candiani, *Dreaming of Dry Land*, 49.

[93] Candiani, *Dreaming of Dry Land*, 50-51, 56-57.

[94] W. Michael Mathes, "To Save a City: The Desagüe of Mexico-Huehuetoca, 1607," *The Americas*, 26, 4 (April, 1970), 419-438, EBSCOhost. Mathes notes that during construction only ten men died from accidents in the tunnel and 63 died of diseases.

walls because they had no revetments. With the tunnel crumbling and water not draining properly, the city's property owners complained that their tax money had been wasted and Indian labor had been commandeered from important agricultural work.[95] These complaints reached Philip III, who in May 1613 asked his ambassador to France to find an engineer who could solved the hydrology issues in Mexico City. Five months later, Adrian Boot, who was paid an alluring hundred ducats a day, arrived in the capital and met with Fernández.[96] The viceroy commissioned a party to escort the Flemish engineer on his inspection of the basin's water management system. After twenty-four days in the field, including a detailed inspection of the tunnel, Boot reported to Fernández that the drainage tunnel project was indeed "a grand work," but that it was "useless for the purpose of freeing the City of Mexico from the risks it faces and the dangers to come." Boot concluded that it would be impossible to drain the lakes of the basin because the cost would be too "extraordinary to be sustainable."[97] As an alternative, Boot proposed that the city invest in a system of twenty new sluice gates and a new eleven-kilometer canal to take water away from the city. He estimated that the canal would cost 340,000 pesos and take three years to complete.[98] Fernández respected Boot's candor and thoroughness, but in January 1615 he rejected the engineer's proposal as impractical because of the political fallout it would generate. The city's elite were vehemently opposed to Boot's plan because of its high costs and the amount of Indian labor it would require.[99] Fernández didn't believe it was prudent to spend the necessary political capital on a project which might or might not work. Such cautiousness generally characterized Fernández's administrative approach as viceroy.[100]

A third issue Fernández dealt with during this time in Mexico, and one that affected him personally, was disease. First came the death in 1613 of the viceroy's oldest daughter, after just a year of life, and then came the death of his wife Mariana, who made her will on February 25, 1619.[101] The viceroy mourned

---

[95] Candiani, *Dreaming of Dry Land*, 62, 64-65.
[96] Rivera Cambas, *Diego Fernández de Córdoba*, 6.
[97] Adrian Boot quoted in Candiani, *Dreaming of Dry Land*, 75-76.
[98] Candiani, *Dreaming of Dry Land*, 76.
[99] Trevino Villarreal, "Diego Fernandez."
[100] Such antipathy for taxes combined with administrative caution had consequences: in 1629 a massive flood kept much of Mexico City underwater for five years. Another example of Fernández's administrative cautiousness involves English incursions into Florida; he waited for a decision from Philip III about how to proceed in Florida, rather than acting on his own as soon as the news reached him. See Rivera Cambas, *Diego Fernández de Córdoba*, 7.
[101] Pérez Herrera, "Diego Fernández de Córdoba y el palacio del marquesado de Guadalcázar." Before she died, Mariana gave birth to three children in Mexico, two girls and a boy. Mariana Manuela was born January 2, 1613 and lived just under a year; Brianda was born January 13,

the loss of his wife deeply. He knew Spanish law prohibited viceroys and other key officials from marrying women within their jurisdictions so as to prevent a concentration of wealth and influence which might undermine royal authority.[102] Fernández was going to be alone for the foreseeable future. He responded to this grief by designing an elaborate funeral to honor Mariana. The arrangements included a protocol-breaking funeral procession and the construction of a platform for her coffin which was larger than the one made for Margaret of Austria in 1611. He also ordered the *oidores* to wear mourning clothes while hearing cases, something which was only normally done upon the death of a king or queen. When this news reached Madrid, the Crown responded negatively, fining Fernández 4,000 ducats for his ceremonial abuses. The viceroy replied to the rebuke, arguing that the colony's remoteness required extra pomp and that he had only been trying to honor the dignity of the viceregal office, not his wife. But in the eyes of most, whether in Mexico City or Madrid, Fernández had gone too far and overstepped his station.[103] He may have been the embodiment of the Crown in New Spain, but he was not the king and Mariana was not the queen.

The rest of the city was certainly not immune from the misfortune that had befallen the viceregal family. The infant mortality rate in the seventeenth century for *Peninsulares* and Creoles was 20%. It was higher for those of mixed race and higher still for Indians.[104] As a result of the Columbian Exchange,* diseases devastated adult populations too. Historians estimate that about 20 million people lived in central Mexico in 1520, but by 1548 there were only six million as the multitudes fell victim to diseases for which they had no immunity.[105] Although no one has found evidence that the Spanish purposefully sought to infect Indians as happened in New England and in the American West, the indigenous population continued to fall through the opening decades of the seventeenth century, as wave after wave of contagions swept across the

---

1614. I have not been able to find an exact birth date for Francisco, but it was between 1614-1619. For confirmation of the girls' birth dates, see Chimalpahin, *Annals of His Time*, 233, 271.
[102] This requirement explains why so many Spanish officials came to the Americas with wives; only merchants were exempt from this rule. It also explains why Fernández never remarried. See María Emma Mannarelli, *Private Passions and Public Sins: Men and Women in Seventeenth Century Lima*, Sidney Evans and Meredith D. Dodge (trans.) (Albuquerque, New Mexico: University of New Mexico Press, 2007), 23, 25.
[103] Cañeque, *The King's Living Image*, 144.
[104] Nicolá Sánchez-Albornoz, "The Population of Colonial Spanish America," *The Cambridge History of Latin America, Volume 2, Colonial Latin America*, Leslie Bethell (ed.) (New York, Cambridge University Press, 1984), 23.
[105] Israel, *Race, Class and Politics in Colonial Mexico, 1610-1670*, 13.

continent.[106] As soon as one disease began to fade away, another followed, with new diseases like yellow fever and malaria entering into the mix. At the same time, the strains of familiar diseases like smallpox and measles became increasingly virulent as time passed, probably as a result of the growth of the Atlantic slave trade.[107] In 1615, for example, smallpox and measles epidemics hit the Valley of Mexico, reaching the highest levels of infection in the first three months of 1616.[108] As with previous episodic arrivals of these diseases, the results were painful to witness. With smallpox, the pustules usually began covering the victim's feet, hands, face, arms and neck, occasionally blending together into a single, massive sore, but in some patients, the legions formed internally, leading to subcutaneous hemorrhaging from the eyes, nose, mouth and anus. In other cases, smallpox victims mysteriously died even before any skin lesions appeared.[109] There was, however, little Fernández or anyone else could do about these horrific epidemics except pray.

The fourth major issue which faced Fernández as viceroy of New Spain was rebellion, and one of the major rebellions during his administration was directly connected to disease. In 1616, the Tepehuan Indians in the Sierra Madre Occidental mountains between Durango and Chihuahua rose up in a rebellion which was thought at the time to be "one of the greatest outbreaks of disorder, upheaval and destruction...seen in New Spain since the Conquest."[110] The Tepehuanes had experienced significant societal stress before the start of seventeenth century, as they, like so many other tribes, had abandoned traditions and beliefs, moved to mission villages, and endured coerced labor. The waves of earlier epidemics had convinced many Tepehuanes that their gods were not powerful enough to stop the widespread deaths, and they had converted to Christianity. With the passage of time, however, the Christian God had proven no more able to terminate the plagues, which hit the Tepehuanes in 1594, 1601-1602, and 1606-1607.[111] In fact, they came to see churches and baptisms by Jesuit

---

[106] David Cook, *Born to Die: Disease and New World Conquest, 1492-1650* (New York: Cambridge University Press, 1998), 214-215. In 1763, for example, Sir Jeffery Amherst advocated for the purposeful infection of Native Americans with smallpox. See Elizabeth A. Fenn, *Pox Americana: The Great Smallpox Epidemic of 1775-82* (New York: Hill and Wang, 2001), 88-89.
[107] Cook, *Born to Die*, 173.
[108] Cook, *Born to Die*, 167. Cook indicates (173) that the repeated outbreaks of smallpox and measles between 1614-1620 is enough to suggest pandemics rather than epidemics.
[109] Fenn, *Pox Americana*, 16-18.
[110] Andrés Pérez De Ribas quoted in Charlotte M. Gradie, *The Tepehuan Revolt of 1616: Militarism, Evangelism, and Colonialism in Seventeenth Century Nueva Vizcaya* (Salt Lake City: University of Utah Press, 2000), 165.
[111] Gradie, *The Tepehuan Revolt of 1616*, 168, 170. Another author cites different dates for the outbreaks: 1590 for smallpox and 1596-1597 for smallpox and measles, but concurs with Gradie

missionaries as the direct cause of death.[112] Then, in 1615, a charismatic shaman named Quautlatas called upon the Tepehuanes to rise up against Spanish for enslaving them. He proclaimed that all Christians had to be killed in order to honor the old Tepehuan gods and that anyone dying in the revolt would be brought back to life. These messages were well received, and by November 1616 the Tepehuanes were ready to strike, having six commanders and key alliances with surrounding tribes.

The coordinated attack on numerous strategic targets resulted in the death of over 200 Spaniards, including eight Jesuits, one Franciscan, and one Dominican, all of whose bodies were mutilated. The Tepehuanes destroyed church altars, flogged statues of the Virgin Mary, urinated on Hosts, drank communion wine, killed livestock, and burned buildings.[113] Spanish commanders in Durango dispatched small contingents of troops as quickly as they learned the news in December 1616. By March 1617 these troops had captured all six of the Tepehuan leaders and put them to death. This brought much of the revolt to a close as Tepehuan allies quickly sued for peace. The entire episode cost the Crown over a million pesos in expenses and loss of revenue from the silver mines; over 300 Spaniards and 1,000 Indians lost their lives.[114] The peace remained tenuous and there were additional Indian revolts later in the century.

The Tepehuan Revolt illustrates both the problems the viceregal government faced in attempting to rule such vast territories and the success it had in doing so. On the one hand, the three companies of soldiers Fernández sent from the capital didn't arrive in Durango until ten months after the rebellion began, while on the other hand Fernández wrote to Philip III to inform him of the situation and to get advice as quickly as he probably could.[115] It took months for Fernández to receive word back from Spain, but when it came Philip made the Spanish position clear: "the uprising must be put down, and if this doesn't happen through the measures taken by the present [provincial] Governor, send someone with more experience for the period of time the war lasts."[116] Fernández, therefore, had to assess the

---

for the events in 1601-1602 (measles, smallpox, and perhaps typhus) and 1606-1607 (measles and smallpox). See Susan M. Deeds, *Defiance and Deference in Mexico's Colonial North: Indians Under Spanish Rule in Nueva Vizcaya* (Austin, Texas: University of Texas Press, 2003), 16.

[112] Susan M. Deeds, "First Generation Rebellions in Seventeenth Century Nueva Vizcaya," *Native Resistance in the Pax Colonial in New Spain*, Susan Schroeder (ed.) (Lincoln, Nebraska: University of Nebraska Press, 1998), 11. Deed's 2003 book cited above puts this rebellion into a broader historical context.

[113] Deeds, "First Generation Rebellions in Seventeenth Century Nueva Vizcaya," 9-10.

[114] Deeds, "First Generation Rebellions in Seventeenth Century Nueva Vizcaya," 11.

[115] The date of Fernández's letter to Philip was February 15, 1617, and the troops arrived in Durango on September 22, 1617. See Gradie, *The Tepehuan Revolt of 1616*, 159, 164.

[116] Philip III quoted in Gradie, *The Tepehuan Revolt of 1616*, 165.

situation, determine the best course of action, restore as much harmony as he could, and balance his dual responsibilities of protecting the Indians and promoting the spread of the Catholic faith. Fernández's decree of January 10, 1618 shows his solution. He ordered that peaceful Indians be treated kindly, and he gave the remaining rebellious Indians a sixty days in which to surrender without facing retribution. Those who failed to accept his offer of amnesty would suffer the consequences.[117] This balanced approach fit with Fernández's political instincts, but also replicated the procedures of the Inquisition when it entered a town to begin its investigations. In the minds of many Spanish administrators, the power to inflict punishment should be moderated by a desire to dispense clemency.[118]

Another rebellion which occurred during Fernández tenure in New Spain involved the viceroyalty's Black population. The status of Blacks was particularly complicated in the Spanish colonies because many were free, many were runaway slaves (known as maroons), and many, whether slave or free, had freedom of movement in places like Mexico City.[119] Spaniards saw owning an African slave as a sign of prestige, but then employed them as overseers for Indian workers and allowed them to purchase their freedom by earning wages.[120] Such

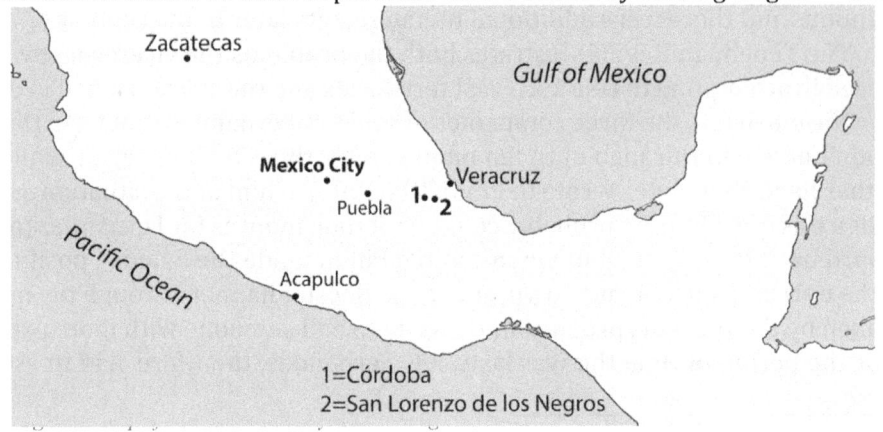

---

[117] Gradie, *The Tepehuan Revolt of 1616*, 165.
[118] Alejandro Cañeque, "The Emotions of Power: Love, Anger, and Fear, or How to Rule the Spanish Empire," *Emotions and Daily Life in Colonial Mexico*, Javier Villa-Flores and Sonya Lipsett-Rivera (ed.) (Albuquerque, New Mexico: University of New Mexico Press, 2014), 103.
[119] Jane G. Landers, "*Cimarrón* and Citizen: African Ethnicity, Corporate Identity, and the Evolution of Free Black Towns in the Spanish Circum-Caribbean," *Slaves, Subjects and Subversives: Blacks in Colonial Latin America*, Jane Landers, and Barry Robinson (eds.) (Albuquerque, New Mexico: University of New Mexico Press, 2006), 119.
[120] Israel, *Race, Class and Politics in Colonial Mexico, 1610-1670*, 72-73.

circumstances did not limit racial tensions between Blacks and Whites. In fact, these tensions were at an all-time high just prior to Fernández's arrival in the colony. In 1611, a Black female slave was flogged to death in Mexico City by her master. The injustice caused more than 1,500 Blacks to join in an organized march in which they carried the woman's body through the streets to the palaces of the archbishop, the Inquisition, the viceroy, and finally to the house of the slave's owner. When the *audiencia* deported the organizer of the march, Blacks began plotting a *coup d'état* for Holy Thursday 1612. Their intent was to replace the viceroy with a Black king and queen.[121] Word of the plot reached colonial authorities, however, and the *audiencia* suspended the Holy Week processions and re-imposed old laws: the dawn-to-dusk curfew for all Blacks, whether slave or free; the ban on carrying weapons; a prohibition on meetings of three or more Blacks at any time; and a rule against wearing luxurious clothing. Then, on May 2, 1612, twenty-nine men and seven women were hanged on nine gallows for their involvement in the plot and their heads were severed and paraded through the streets on pikes to warn other Blacks from rebellion.[122] By the time Fernández arrived in Mexico City that fall, Spanish ardor had cooled, but as his term progressed new tensions arose.

The greatest of these were the return of maroon raids on the vital Veracruz-Mexico City road and an uprising by maroons in 1617-1618. Like several of his predecessors, Fernández dispatched troops to restore order, but as in the past his military commanders found it impossible to combat the guerrilla-style warfare of the maroons in the mountains. In the end, the Spanish simply renewed an existing agreement with the maroon leader Yanga: in exchange for their freedom and independence from Spanish harassment, the maroons would stop raiding the Veracruz-Mexico City road and return any new runaway slaves who attempted to join their community. This time, however, the Spanish also formally recognized the right of the Blacks to have a permanent town with their own *cabildo*. The town took the name San Lorenzo de los Negros.[123] Fernández then granted the Black community sufficient lands surrounding San Lorenzo to support the town. As an additional precaution, in 1618 Fernández founded the Spanish town of Córdoba in the heart of maroon territory so Spanish troops could protect supply routes and watch for runaway slaves.[124] By the end of his term as viceroy of New

---

[121] Landers, "*Cimarrón* and Citizen," 119-120.
[122] Israel, *Race, Class and Politics in Colonial Mexico, 1610-1670*, 70-71.
[123] Today the town is called Yanga in honor of the maroon leader.
[124] Jane G. Landers, "*Cimarrón* and Citizen: African Ethnicity, Corporate Identity, and the Evolution of Free Black Towns in the Spanish Circum-Caribbean," *Slaves, Subjects and Subversives: Blacks in Colonial Latin America*, Jane Landers, and Barry Robinson (ed.) (Albuquerque, New Mexico: University of New Mexico Press, 2006), 125-128. Yanga, who claimed to be an African

Spain, relations between Whites and Blacks were far less tense than when Fernández took office.

Despite his even-handed approach to viceregal administration and a reasonable record of accomplishment (including the establishment of colleges and the construction of a 900-arch aqueduct), Fernández's term ended ignominiously: his *audiencia* staged a *coup d'état* against him. Its members may have had authorization from Spain, but it is more likely that they acted on their own, realizing that with Philip III's impending death Fernández would lose the basis of his support in Madrid. Fernández had certainly made enemies. He had, for example, angered Archbishop Pérez de la Serna and violated direct orders from the court by refusing to allow the archbishop to evaluate the competence of the assistants to parish priests who were members of religious orders. In January 1620, the members of the *audiencia* began virulently attacking what they described as Fernández's "tyrannical" rule.[125] The viceroy's last day in office was March 14, 1621.[126]

What happened next is unclear because Fernández didn't arrive in Lima to begin his term as the viceroy of Peru for sixteen months after being removed from office in Mexico City. He probably lived in Mexico City as a private citizen, awaiting news of a new appointment from Philip IV.[127] At some point, he made his way to Acapulco, accompanied by his two surviving children, a boy and a girl. Once in Acapulco, Fernández saw the impressive, five-bastion* fortress of San Diego for the first time. How ironic the structure must have seemed to the viceroy, who in an effort to secure the Manila trade in the face of new Dutch encroachments into the Pacific, had authorized the fort's construction in 1615 without waiting for approval or financial support from Spain.[128] Designed by

---

chief, began his community in the 1570s in the mountains west of Veracruz. Yanga and followers lived in settled, agricultural communities for almost forty years before the founding of San Lorenzo de los Negros.

[125] Israel, *Race, Class and Politics in Colonial Mexico, 1610-1670*, 137, 141.

[126] The next viceroy, Marques de Gelves, arrived in New Spain in 1621 on a mission to end corruption. As a result of his authoritarian style, Gelves quickly alienated the archbishop, the members of the *audiencia*, and the merchant community. He was ousted from office in 1624.

[127] Israel, *Race, Class and Politics in Colonial Mexico, 1610-1670*, 137. This appointment came as the result of Fernández's having sufficiently pleased royal officials in Spain during his tenure as viceroy of New Spain. See Rivera Cambas, *Diego Fernández de Córdoba*, 17.

[128] The Dutch captain Joris Van Spilbergen's fleet of five ships, 150 guns and 800 men entered the Pacific and defeated the Spanish off the coast of Peru on July 17-18, 1615. Spilbergen proceeded north, arriving in Acapulco on October 11, 1615, where he agreed to exchange fresh provisions and prisoners instead of destroying the town. Later, Spilbergen sailed for the Moluccas having never encountered the Manila galleons, but his appearance prompted Fernández's actions and the fort's construction. See Engel Sluiter, "The Fortification of

Adrian Boot and erected in just seven months, the fort dominated the entire crescent moon harbor. It undoubtedly stood in Fernández's mind as a symbol of effective leadership. Yet he was leaving Mexico under a cloud without the pomp that had greeted him upon his arrival. He could take some comfort in the fact that he had an even more prestigious appointment awaiting him.

∼

Ynes Quispi's simple canopy in the market in the Plaza Mayor faced both Lima's newly-completed cathedral with its two rather squat bell towers and three great portals, and the archbishop's residence, which a Jesuit described in 1629 as having "splendid windows." To her left stood "the largest and most luxurious structure" in the kingdom, the viceregal palace, which was "resplendent" despite having only one story. Behind Quispi, on the west side of the square, rose the "imposing and magnificent" town hall for the *cabildos*; to her right stood a row of commercial buildings "featuring stone columns, a brick arcade and many large balconies with windows." The market offered "anything a well-supplied republic could desire for its sustenance and comfort," while surrounding stores specialized in the fashionable goods Lima's elite sought.[129] Quispi's simple produce and clothing stand might not look like much, but its simplicity belied both her personal ambition and her overall economic importance to the community.

Quispi was an Andean woman from the highlands about a hundred miles southeast of Lima. Although illiterate, she owned land in the countryside and a house in the city, managed a business, employed at least one person in Lima to help her sell her goods, and understood Spanish property law quite thoroughly.[130] Quispi raised fruits and vegetables on land outside of Lima she and her husband worked together, but her will of 1623 makes it clear that she saw herself as an independent economic entity, noting the amount of money she put into the business over the years and the amount of her original dowry. She also owned a large amount of high-quality clothing. Documenting her financial status was

---

Acapulco, 1615-1616," *The Hispanic American Historical Review*, 29, 1 (February, 1949), 69-80, EBSCOhost.

[129] Bernabé Cobo, "Viceregal Lima in the Seventeenth Century," *I Saw a City Invincible: Urban Portraits of Latin America*, Sharon Kellum (trans.) (Wilmington, Delaware, 1996), 62-63. Cobo wrote his account of the history of Lima between 1611-1639; this description of the Plaza Mayor is from 1629.

[130] Graubart, *With Our Labor and Sweat*, 70-72. All of the subsequent information on Quispi also comes from these pages.

important to Quispi because she also served as an unofficial financier for many of the other vendors on the Plaza Mayor.

One can imagine Quispi surveying the market scene one crisp morning as *limeños* began their day. It was a busy place, for in the words of one early seventeenth century commentator, "everyone [in Lima] is a merchant, even if it is through a third party or on the sly."[131] Quispi easily could have chatted with an Andean woman under the awning on her left or with a free Black woman under the canopy on her right, for all of these women were members of a shared economic community with social ties.[132] In fact, they probably lived as neighbors in Lima's largest parish, where in 1619 women composed 38% of the parish's Andean population, and 46% of its Black population.[133] As for social and economic interactions, any of these women might have hired a Black slave as a day laborer since it was common for slaves to work for wages, give a percentage of their wages to their masters, and keep the rest so that in time they could buy their freedom.[134] Alternatively, these women might have had an apprentice.[135] The Iberian men who owned the stores may have dominated the highest levels of Lima's commerce, but the things of everyday life were sold by women like Quispi, utilizing multiethnic networks.[136]

Other people would have caught Quispi's eye that morning: the elite Spanish women carried in sedan chairs through the streets[137] or the multitude of shoppers, noble or not, who would spend "incredible sums" on "all kinds of silks, fabrics, brocades, delicate linens and fine textiles" since there was "no moderation at all in this part of the world."[138] There were carpenters and silversmiths, orphans and vagabonds, government officials and priests. There were also seductively posed, flirtatious women looking out from wood-latticed

---

[131] Anonymous, "Pedro de León Portocarrero's Description of Lima Peru," *Colonial Latin America: A Documentary History*, Kenneth Mills, William B. Taylor and Sandra Lauderdale Graham (ed.) (Wilmington, Delaware: Scholarly Resources, Inc., 2002), 193. As the editors note, the text was not signed, but many historians believe that the description of Lima was authored by Pedro de León Portocarrero, a *converso* who hid his identity to emigrate to the Americas.

[132] Graubart, *With Our Labor and Sweat*, 90.

[133] María Emma Mannarelli, *Private Passions and Public Sins: Men and Women in Seventeenth Century Lima*, Sidney Evans and Meredith D. Dodge (trans.) (Albuquerque, New Mexico: University of New Mexico Press, 2007), 20.

[134] Henry Louis Gates, Jr., *Blacks in Latin America* (New York: New York University Press, 2011), 96.

[135] Graubart, *With Our Labor and Sweat*, 92.

[136] Graubart, *With Our Labor and Sweat*, 70.

[137] Graubart, *With Our Labor and Sweat*, 87.

[138] Bernabé Cobo, "Viceregal Lima in the Seventeenth Century," 67-68.

balconies or riding in carriages or simply walking down the street, their heads wrapped up so a passerby could only see one eye.

These women were not prostitutes. They were *tapadas*: women dressed in the most expensive fashions, purposely showing the lace of their undergarments; they used a shawl to conceal their identity and maintain their anonymity so that they might break social conventions and do as they pleased.[139] Some saw their mystery as defining sexual desirability. Others saw their unrecognizability as a threat to social order in a racially diverse, economically stratified city. If husbands couldn't identify their own wives, if fathers couldn't recognize their own daughters, if men could dress as women without anyone knowing, then the value of Christian modesty signified little.[140] This is why, soon after his arrival in Lima as the new viceroy, Fernández de Córdoba found himself beseeched by male petitioners to do something about what they described as the social menace of the *tapada*. These petitioners had not had viceregal support in the past. One of Fernández's predecessors argued that "since I have seen that each husband cannot control his own wife, I have no confidence whatsoever that I will be able

Figure 7: "A Woman Wearing the Saya and Manto Standing in Profile, from a Group of Drawings Depicting Peruvian Costume," watercolor by Francisco (Pancho) Fierro, 1848, courtesy of the Metropolitan Museum of Art, New York, 38.145.464.

---

[139] Luis Martín, *Daughters of the Conquistadors: Women of the Viceroyalty of Peru* (Dallas, Texas: Southern Methodist University, 1983), 281, 299.
[140] Laura R. Bass, Amanda Wunder and Enrique Garcia Santo-Tomás, "The Veiled Ladies of the Early Modern Spanish World: Seduction and Scandal in Seville, Madrid and Lima," *Hispanic Review*, 27.1 (2009), 97-146, ProQuest Central.

to control all of them together."[141] Fernández felt an obligation to try to address a situation that had the potential to create unruliness. He issued an ordinance that as of December 10, 1624, all women, regardless of class or whereabouts, had to leave their faces "uncovered so that they may be seen and recognized at all times."[142] Read in every Peruvian town, the ordinance specified punishments, which were substantially harsher than any previously issued for the offense. All women found in violation would be fined sixty pesos, but the prison terms differed by race and class; noble women faced a prison term of ten days, while Black and mixed race women faced prison terms of thirty days.[143] Those who were found guilty of a second violation were to be banished from their communities for a year.[144] These punishments did not, however, provide a sufficient deterrent for Peruvian women. The *tapadas* tradition continued well into the nineteenth century.

The status of every Peruvian viceroy ultimately rested upon something far more material and tangible than divergent social mores: the amount of silver transported from the colony to Spain. Most of this metal came from Potosí, a single 15,800-foot mountain in modern Bolivia which contained one of the world's largest concentrations of silver ore. Between 1574 and 1735, miners extracted almost 20,000 tons of silver from Potosí.[145] The Crown took one fifth of the production, which it used to help finance its military needs and defend Catholicism around the globe. The supply of silver from Potosí was essential because its liquidity allowed Spain to pay its troops and obtain necessary loans.[146] This is why Fernández received such acclaim for successfully defending Lima's port of Callao in the face of a Dutch attack in 1624. It is also why it was fortuitous that he had ordered the Spanish treasure fleet carrying nine million pesos of silver to depart Callao for Panama just five days before the Dutch arrived.[147] Potosí's silver was Spain's lifeblood.

---

[141] Juan de Mendoza y Luna, Marquess of Montesclaros, quoted in Martín, *Daughters of the Conquistador*, 303.
[142] Diego Fernández de Córdoba quoted in Martín, *Daughters of the Conquistadors*, 304.
[143] Bass, Wunder and Garcia Santo-Tomás, "The Veiled Ladies of the Early Modern Spanish World."
[144] Martín, *Daughters of the Conquistadors*, 304.
[145] Nicolas A. Robin and Nicole A. Hagan, "Mercury Production and Use in Colonial Andean Silver Production: Emissions and Health Implications," *Environmental Health Perspectives*, 120.5 (May 2012), 627-31, ProQuest Central. This includes the 25% presumably lost to contraband. Significantly, this huge influx of specie into the European economy created inflation; when silver supplies began to shrink, the Spanish economy contracted.
[146] Elliott, "Spain and America in the Sixteenth and Seventeenth Centuries," 322.
[147] Lynch, *Spain Under the Habsburgs, Volume II: Spain and America, 1598-1700*, 181. The Dutch never caught the Spanish treasure fleet, partially because they attacked Guayaquil. Interestingly,

35

Figure 8: "View of Potosí," print by Thomas Doesburgh, before 1714, courtesy of Rijksmuseum, Amsterdam, RP-P-1889-A-15214.

The production of ore necessary for these coins came at a significant human cost. Because all of the easily accessible ore had been removed from Potosí by 1572, Viceroy Francisco de Toledo had created a compulsory Andean labor system to extract silver. This system was called the *mita*. Pressed into service as vassals to the crown, all Andean men between eighteen and fifty who lived in one of sixteen high-altitude provinces had to report to Potosí once every seven years for a twelve-month contract. This system created a workforce of 13,500 laborers, who worked in one-week shifts followed by two weeks of rest. Originally, workers received wages, had the costs of transportation to Potosí funded, and worked from dawn to dusk Tuesday through Saturday, spending their nights

---

when this fleet reached Acapulco in October 1624, Fernández's and Adrian Boot's fort there withstood the attack. Perhaps as a result of his experiences with rebellion in Mexico, as part of the preparations to defend Lima Fernández established a regiment of Black mercenaries to put down any Andean or Black rebellion in the moment of crisis. See Benjamin Schmidt, "Exotic Allies: the Dutch-Chilean Encounter and the (Failed) Conquest of America," *Renaissance Quarterly*, 52.2 (1999), 440-473, ProQuest Central.

above ground.[148] This system was prone to significant abuse. Men were forced, for example, to stay in the mines overnight or were beaten to meet illegal production quotas.[149] Whereas Toledo had specified that miners could only make two trips hauling rock out of the mines a day, by the 1590s the Andean miners regularly carried nineteen. The conditions were horrific, as noted by a priest in the 1590s:

> They labor in these mines in perpetual darkness, not knowing day from night. And since the sun never penetrates to these places...the air is very thick and alien to the nature of men....The ore is generally hard as flint, and they break it up with iron bars. They carry the ore on their backs up ladders made of three cords of twisted rawhide joined by pieces of wood that serve as rungs....Each man usually carries on his back a load of [fifty-five pounds] of silver ore tied in a cloth, knapsack fashion....They climb a great distance, often more than [980 feet]—a fearful thing, the mere thought of which inspires dread.[150]

Once the rock was on the surface, it went to one of the 124 refineries located in the town at the base of the mountain, where it was crushed into the consistency of flour. Once sufficiently ground, Andeans then mixed a combination of copper pyrite, salt, and mercury into the rock and ore with their bare legs for six to eight weeks so that the mercury would amalgamate with the silver. Once the silver and the mercury were sufficiently integrated, the composition was shoveled into vats and washed to carry off the waste rock. The remaining silver and mercury were then heated to allow the mercury to evaporate, leaving pure silver and creating toxic clouds of vapor.[151]

The conditions were so bad that Andeans went to great lengths to avoid the Potosí *mita* altogether. They ran away from the towns they had been assigned to live in by colonial officials or hired replacements to fulfill their service. Andeans who survived their first tour of duty frequently stayed in Potosí and found less-

---

[148] Peter Bakewell, "Mining in Colonial Spain America," *The Cambridge History of Latin America, Volume 2, Colonial Latin America*, Leslie Bethell (ed.) (New York, Cambridge University Press, 1984), 124-125. One historian notes that in Toledo's tenure, the *mita* was a widely-praised solution to the labor issues and became so embedded that it lasted until 1825, when Simón Bolívar finally ended it. See Kris Lane, *Potosí: The Silver City that Changed the World* (Oakland, California: University of California Press, 2019), 71-72.
[149] Kenneth J. Andrien, *Andean Worlds: Indigenous History, Culture and Consciousness Under Spanish Rule, 1532-1825* (Albuquerque, New Mexico, University of New Mexico Press, 2001), 61.
[150] Jeffery A. Cole, *The Potosí Mita, 1573-1700: Compulsive Labor in the Andes* (Stanford, California: Stanford University Press, 1985), 24.
[151] Bakewell, "Mining in Colonial Spain America," 115-116.

risky work as wage employees to avoid the jobs assigned to those under the *mita* contract.[152] Some even went further: a mid-seventeenth century report noted that "many mothers maim their infant sons in the arms or legs so that when they are older they will be exempt" from *mita* service, especially if they thought that service would be in the deadly mercury mines of Huancavelica.[153]

Fernández became convinced early in this term that the Potosí *mita* was an unsustainable enterprise. Analyzing the data available to him, he concluded that the towns of the high Andean plain could not support the required draft numbers for very much longer. Consequently, Fernández wrote to Philip IV, urging the Crown to reduce the number of required draftees, regardless of the effects on silver production. Surprisingly, but echoing both his father's and his grandfather's concern for the indigenous peoples of the Americas, Philip IV agreed to Fernández's proposal. This royal agreement should have produced a dramatic change in the *mita* system, but when he got the news from Madrid, Fernández wavered: he decided to wait for individual communities to request a reassessment of their *mita* quotas instead of making a sweeping directive.[154]

Fernández's hesitancy rested in his fear of disorder, and this fear had some justification. In 1618, a civil war broke out in Potosí after years of bitter animosity between the Spanish and the Basques, who owned most of the mines and dominated the *cabildo*, mint, and royal treasury.[155] According to one contemporary account, the Basques lorded their position and wealth over everyone else in Potosí, treating all others "disdainfully and vituperously."[156] The Spaniards, both *Peninsulares* and Creoles, resented the Basques' status and resorted to violence. Between 1622 and 1624, five thousand people died in their

---

[152] By 2010, so much rock and ore had been removed from the mountain that a sinkhole began opening near the summit, risking the collapse of tunnels far below. In June 2014, UNESCO warned that the summit was in danger of collapse, threatening the still-operating mine shafts below. The following month, the Bolivian government moved to close mines above 14,435 feet, but miners continue to work there under brutal conditions. See William Neuman, "For Miners, Increasing Risk on a Mountain at the Heart of Bolivia's Identity," *The New York Times*, September 16, 2014, A9, ProQuest Historical Newspapers. Attempts to regulate conditions have not been effective. See Kenneth Dickerman and Simone Francescangeli, "What Life is Like for the Teenage Miners of Potosi, Bolivia," *The Washington Post*, 2018, ProQuest Central.
[153] Ann M. Wightman, *Indigenous Migration and Social Change: The Forasteros of Cuzco, 1570-1720* (Durham, North Carolina: Duke University Press, 1990), 50.
[154] Cole, *The Potosí Mita, 1573-1700*, 77-78.
[155] Kris Lane, *Potosí: The Silver City that Changed the World* (Oakland, California: University of California Press, 2019), 113. Lane notes that the animosity between then Spanish and the Basques also stemmed from long-standing rivalries in peninsular Spain.
[156] William A. Douglass and Jon Bilbao, *Amerikanuak: Basques in the New World* (Reno, Nevada, University of Nevada Press, 2005), 82.

conflict. This level of bloodshed between Whites in the Spanish colonies was unprecedented. It is possible that the conflict went beyond ethnic and financial jealousy: the violence may have actually been a consequence of widespread mercury poisoning.[157] Whatever the cause, the violence became so disruptive that Fernández traveled to Potosí in 1624 to negotiate a settlement, rather than send a subordinate as would have been customary.[158] Fernández believed that the peace settlement he negotiated favored both sides equally.[159] It provided for the marriage of a Castilian girl to the son of a Basque leader, thereby helping to restore honor and soothe ethnic tensions,[160] but the consequences of visible unrest between Whites threatened the social fabric of Peru; this was something Fernández could not risk any more than he could gamble on the flow of silver from Potosí. In the end, Spain's goal of protecting the indigenous population of the Americas was incompatible with its goal of combating the twin evils of Islam and Protestantism in the late sixteenth and early seventh century; it needed the wealth of the mines to pay for the armies to fight the English, the Dutch, and Ottomans, and the only way to operate them efficiently was with indigenous labor. Old World realities trumped New World aspirations.

Ironically, the opposite was true in the Andeans' practice of Catholicism: New World realities trumped Old World aspirations. By the time Fernández arrived in Peru in 1621, a rigorous campaign against idolatry, superstition, and witchcraft had been underway for a dozen years. It began with great enthusiasm in Lima in 1609, where an *auto-de-fé* resulted in the beating of an Andean shaman and the burning of idols and ancestral mummies just before Christmas. In subsequent years, the clergy became deeply divided as to the campaign's merits and necessity, partly because it utilized the procedures of the Inquisition. The most ardent proponents of the campaign believed that the Andeans were "so persistent in their idolatry that almost all of them have relapsed into paganism."[161] These clerics argued that it was appropriate to instill "fear and terror" in the Andeans in order to end this "plague."[162] At the other end of the spectrum, the provincial of the Augustinians stated that "not even a trace" of idolatry could be found in his

---

[157] Robin and Hagan, "Mercury Production and Use in Colonial Andean Silver Production."
[158] Fisher, *Viceregal Administration in the Spanish-American Colonies*, 257.
[159] Diego Fernández de Córdoba, Marqués de Guadalcázar in *Colección de las Memorias o Relaciones que Escribieron los Virreyes del Perú Acerca del Estado en que Dejaban Las Cosas Generales del Reino*, Tomo 11 (Madrid, Spain: Imprenta Mujeres Españolas, MCMXXX (1930)), 226.
[160] Douglass and Bilbao, *Amerikanuak: Basques in the New World*, 82-83.
[161] Anonymous letter quoted in Joseph de Arriaga, *The Extirpation of Idolatry in Peru*, L. Clark Keating (ed. and trans.) (Lexington, Kentucky, University of Kentucky Press, 1968), 140.
[162] Gonzalo de Campo quoted in Nicolas Griffiths, *The Cross and the Serpent: Religious Repression and Resurgence in Colonial Peru* (Norman, Oklahoma: University of Oklahoma Press, 1996), 36.

jurisdiction,[163] and the bishops of Arequipa and Trujillo argued that even if idolatry could be found, the appropriate response was preaching and education, not torture.[164] In reality, there was an incompleteness to the Andeans' Christianization, but there was also a significant incorporation of Catholic ritual and belief. This was possible because priests sought to utilize native religiosity, carefully substituted local deities for Christian figures, and encouraged the blending of Andean and European clothing in religious festivals.[165] Indeed, many Andeans in the seventeenth century enthusiastically participated in Catholic festivals and ceremonies and readily used Catholic prayers and devotional objects, but they also honored their cultural past by continuing to worship local deities and to venerate their ancestors in customary ways.[166] While there were those who refused to accept Spanish rule and culture well into the seventeenth century, in most regions a blending of religious traditions occurred.[167] One example is the way the Andean Earth Mother goddess, Pachamama, became transformed into the Virgin Mary.[168] For his part, Fernández saw himself as the "healer and protector" of the Andeans and stated that their conversion and education was one of his most important obligations as viceroy. This belief led him to establish new schools and to urge the Crown to continue financing idolatry inspections.[169] A strong indication of Fernández's sense of moderation rests in the fact that the periods of the idolatry campaign's greatest intensity came before and after his term as viceroy.[170] Indeed, Fernández's held the same general

---

[163] Francisco de la Serna quoted in Griffiths, *The Cross and the Serpent*, 56.
[164] Griffiths, *The Cross and the Serpent*, 56-59.
[165] Carolyn Dean, *Inka Bodies and the Body of Christ: Corpus Christi in Colonial Cuzco, Peru* (Durham, North Carolina: Duke University Press, 1999), 16, 122, 159.
[166] Kenneth J. Andrien, *Andean Worlds: Indigenous History, Culture and Consciousness Under Spanish Rule, 1532-1825* (Albuquerque, New Mexico, University of New Mexico Press, 2001), 154-160, 190-191.
[167] The Araucanian Indians of Chile, for example, persisted in a guerrilla war against the Spanish deep into the colonial period. Fernández's nephew, Luis Fernández de Córdoba y Arce, became the governor of Chile in 1625 and despite his ruthless attempts to subjugate the indigenous people, Luis had no more success in reaching his goals than either his predecessors or his successors. See Brian Loveman, *Chile: The Legacy of Hispanic Capitalism* (New York: Oxford University Press, 1979), 65-66.
[168] Carol Damian, *The Virgin of the Andes: Art and Ritual in Colonial Cuzco* (Miami Beach, Florida: Grassfield Press, 1995), 26.
[169] Fernández de Córdoba, *Colección de las Memorias o Relaciones que Escribieron los Virreyes del Perú Acerca del Estado en que Dejaban Las Cosas Generales del Reino*, 238, 268-269.
[170] The periods of greatest intensity were 1609-1622 and 1649-1670. During Fernández's term, there was one year of intense extirpation (1625-1626), created by the appointment of a new archbishop, who died soon into his term. See Griffiths, *The Cross and the Serpent*, 10, and Andrien, *Andean Worlds*, 154-160, 173-177.

attitude toward the idolatry campaign in Peru that he had held towards the Inquisition in Mexico.

Some of the best evidence of the syncretism which emerged in the Spanish colonies can be found in a large painting hanging prominently in the cathedral in Cuzco, Peru. Painted by Marcos Zapata in the mid-eighteenth century, *The Last Supper* merges conventional Christian iconography with Andean customs. Jesus and the Apostles sit around a rectangular table with only Judas looking away from Christ. Judas bears a clear resemblance to conquistador Francisco Pizarro and holds a bag of money under the table. Instead of the bread and the wine being the focus of their meal, a cooked guinea pig rests on its back on a large platter in the middle of the table. The guinea pig, or *cuy*, was an important source of protein in the Andean diet, as well as an important element in Incan religious rituals; it was frequently used as a sacrificial offering.[171] The *cuy*'s inclusion in the painting, hung in a Baroque church situated on the site of an important Incan temple, shows how Andean beliefs and practices were not completely supplanted by Catholicism, despite the campaigns against idolatry. In the long run, the Church learned that the best way for Christianity to become meaningful in the Andes was to accommodate local sensibilities while remaining true to its fundamental tenets.[172] Only in this way could Philip II's vision of a great Catholic empire in the New World become a reality.

~

After sixteen years of service to the Crown in the Americas, Diego Fernández de Córdoba wrote to Philip IV, asking for permission to return to Spain. He wanted to retire. He wanted to enjoy the luxurious palace constructed for him in the Andalusian town of Guadalcázar while he was in the New World.[173] In his

---

[171] Allison Lee Palmer, "The Last Supper by Marcos Zapata (c. 1753): A Meal of Bread, Wine, and Guinea Pig," *Aurora, The Journal of the History of Art*, 9 (Annual, 2008), 54+, EBSCOhost.
[172] Gabriela Ramos, *Death and Conversion in the Andes: Lima and Cuzco, 1532-1670* (Notre Dame, Indiana: University of Notre Dame Press, 2010), 222. Similarly, in Mexico, beatification of Fray Felipe de Jesús de las Casas, the first saint from the Americas, offered colonial leaders the chance to celebrate Mexico's contributions to the Empire and the Catholic Church, while accommodating local sensibilities. See Conover, *Pious Imperialism*, 61, 64, 83.
[173] Pérez Herrera, "Diego Fernández de Córdoba y el palacio del marquesado de Guadalcázar." Financing for the palace largely came from the wealth Fernández accumulated as viceroy, which is why many historians accuse him of considerable corruption. J. H. Elliot says, for example, that during Fernández's administration of New Spain, "government was lax, corruption rampant, and

summary account of his time in Peru, Fernández indicated that he had done his best to improve upon what he had found during his tenure.[174] The king granted Fernández's request, and in January 1629, the viceroy sailed for home with his teenage children, Brianda and Francisco. Fernández died just twenty-two months later, in October 1630, at the age of fifty-two, not having enjoyed his newly-constructed palace for very long.

It is easy to find zealots in the pages of history, but Fernández does not stand as one of them. A dutiful bureaucrat for the Spanish Crown, he liked constancy and order so much that he told his successor in Lima, "As you now enter government, it would be better not to make any innovations in these regulations until, having more experience, you can consult with the King" about them.[175] This may not make Fernández a particularly exciting or morally righteous figure, but he also didn't persecute or abuse those he governed. Unlike those more famous in the sixteenth and seventeenth centuries, he was a cautious and prudent man, who seemed to understand human frailties and to have the capacity to work with them. Never dogmatic or totalitarian, Fernández wouldn't have been particularly troubled by the appearance of the guinea pig in *The Last Supper*, even if he would have strongly objected to any association between the deeds of Judas and those of Pizarro.

---

collusion between royal officials and a handful of leading families led to the further enrichment of a privileged few." See Elliott, "Spain and America in the Sixteenth and Seventeenth Centuries," 317.

[174] Fernández de Córdoba, *Colección de las Memorias o Relaciones que Escribieron los Virreyes del Perú Acerca del Estado en que Dejaban Las Cosas Generales del Reino*, 216.

[175] Diego Fernández de Córdoba quoted in Wightman, *Indigenous Migration and Social Change*, 37.

Glossary:

BASTION: A part of a fortress which projects out from its main walls and which offers additional firing angles for the defenders in a siege.

COLUMBIAN EXCHANGE: A term for the plants, animals, and diseases that were transferred from the Americas to Europe and Africa and vice versa as a result of European ships traveling across the Atlantic Ocean in the late fifteenth and sixteenth centuries. Examples of the Exchange include cacao, maize, potatoes, tobacco, and probably syphilis traveling *from* the Americas; and coffee, horses, measles, smallpox, sugarcane, and African slaves traveling *to* the Americas.

GUILDS: The medieval and early modern associations of artisans and craftsmen that established standards for a particular trade and trained apprentices in the profession.

MERCANTILISM: An economic theory that holds that careful regulation, instead of free trade, is the best way to maximize profits and growth for one nation while simultaneously taking away profits from competing countries.

PAPAL NUNCIO: The Vatican's ambassador to another nation.

PURGATORY: A state of being after death in which humans pay for their earthly sins before gaining admission to Heaven.

SCHOLASTICISM: A medieval method of didactic investigation which critically examined theological questions through specific rules of inquiry and discussion in an attempt to reconcile reason and revelation.

Suggested Reading:

Buschmann, Rainer F., Edward R. Slack Jr., and James B. Tueller. *Navigating the Spanish Lake: The Pacific in the Iberian World, 1521-1898*. Honolulu, Hawai'i: University of Hawai'i Press, 2013.
Candiani, Vera S. *Dreaming of Dry Land: Environmental Transformation in Colonial Mexico City*. Stanford, California: Stanford University Press, 2014.
Cañeque, Alejandro. *The King's Living Image: The Culture and Politics of Viceregal Power in Colonial Mexico*. New York: Routledge, 2004.
Conover, Cornelius. *Pious Imperialism: Spanish Rule and the Cult of the Saints in Mexico City*. Albuquerque, New Mexico: University of New Mexico Press, 2019.
Curcio-Nagy, Linda A., *The Great Festivals of Colonial Mexico City: Performing Power and Identity*. Albuquerque, New Mexico: University of New Mexico Press, 2004.
Gates, Jr., Henry Louis. *Blacks in Latin America*. New York: New York University Press, 2011.
Lane, Kris. *Potosí: The Silver City that Changed the World*. Oakland, California: University of California Press, 2019.
Lowney, Chris. *A Vanished World: Muslims, Christians, and Jews in Medieval Spain*. New York: Oxford University Press, 2006.
Mannarelli, María Emma. *Private Passions and Public Sins: Men and Women in Seventeenth Century Lima*. Albuquerque, New Mexico: University of New Mexico Press, 2007.
Nesvig, Martin Austin. *Ideology and Inquisition: The World of the Censors in Early Mexico*. New Haven, Connecticut: Yale University Press, 2009.
Silverblatt, Irene. *Modern Inquisitions: Peru and the Colonial Origins of the Civilized World*. Durham, North Carolina: Duke University Press, 2004.
Villa-Flores, Javier and Sonya Lipsett-Rivera (eds.) *Emotions and Daily Life in Colonial Mexico*. Albuquerque, New Mexico: University of New Mexico Press, 2014.